PERCEPTUAL STIMULI

Perceptual Stimuli

TONY MEDLEY

MEDLEY

CONTENTS

~ *VII*

~11~

Experience Great & Mighty Things
60

PREFACE

This book was born out of countless moments of prayer, meditation, and a relentless pursuit of hearing the voice of God more clearly. I have come to realize that the Christian journey is not merely about attending services, quoting scriptures, or carrying titles. It is about perception—a divinely stimulated awareness of what God is doing, what He is saying, and how He is moving in the earth today.

Too often, believers miss the fullness of their destiny because their spiritual senses remain underdeveloped. We settle for the natural when God has called us to live by revelation. We repeat yesterday's patterns, unaware that God is ushering us into today's miracles. This book was written to challenge that cycle and to ignite your ability to live with awakened perception.

As you turn these pages, you will see that every chapter is both practical and prophetic. You will be stretched to believe bigger, to trust deeper, and to discern sharper. My prayer is that this work will not just inform your mind, but also transform your life—causing you to rise into your divine calling with clarity, courage, and conviction.

This is not simply another Christian teaching. It is an invitation to live life at God's frequency.

— Dr. Tony E. Medley Sr.

FOREWORD

We live in a world overflowing with noise. The constant hum of technology, the demands of survival, and the distractions of culture compete for our attention. Yet, in the midst of all of this, God continues to speak. He speaks through His Word, His Spirit, His creation, and even through the circumstances of life. The question is not if God is speaking—the question is are we perceiving?

Perceptual Stimuli is about tuning in to the frequency of Heaven. It is about training your spiritual senses to pick up divine signals in everyday life. Just as our natural senses allow us to navigate the physical world, our spiritual senses allow us to navigate the unseen. When these senses are awakened by the Spirit, we gain access to strategies, revelations, and insights that cannot be learned in classrooms or boardrooms, but only in the presence of God.

This book is not for casual readers; it is for hungry believers. It is for those who sense that God has more, that there is another level, that destiny is calling louder than fear. Each chapter will draw you deeper into the mystery of God's wisdom and position you to live as one who discerns, decides, and dominates by revelation.

By the time you reach the final chapter, my prayer is that you will no longer live as a reactor to life's events but as a conductor of Kingdom outcomes. You will know what it means to be led, guarded, and propelled by the Spirit of the Living God.

Welcome to a life of Great and Mighty Things.

DEDICATION

Every generation needs a voice that calls believers higher—a voice that refuses to let the Church settle for the ordinary when God has destined us for the extraordinary. In Perceptual Stimuli, Dr. Tony E. Medley Sr. has released such a voice.

This work is both timely and timeless. It is timely because our present age is clouded with distractions, deception, and division—requiring believers who can cut through the noise with spiritual clarity. And it is timeless because the call to discern, to walk by faith, and to perceive the movement of God has always been the true mark of those who follow Him.

What you will encounter in these chapters is not mere theory; it is revelation forged in the crucible of experience, prayer, and faith. Dr. Medley does not simply write as a teacher—he writes as one who has walked this journey and invites you to do the same.

If you desire to break free from cycles of confusion, fear, and limitation, and if you are ready to step into a dimension of victory, purpose, and divine insight, then this book is your guide. Approach it prayerfully. Read it attentively. Apply it boldly. And watch as your life is transformed from ordinary perception into extraordinary revelation.

This is more than a book—it is a manual for living at Heaven's frequency.

PART I – FOUNDATIONS OF PERCEPTION

~ 1 ~

A LIFE FULL OF INCREDIBLE OUTCOMES

"But without faith it is impossible to please Him, for he that comes to God must believe that He is, and that He is a rewarder of those who diligently seek Him." – Hebrews 11:6

Faith: The Key to Perceiving God

We must know that we cannot perceive what God is doing unless we have faith in what He is able to do. Faith is not a mere mental agreement, nor is it shallow optimism. Faith is the ability to be persuaded of the truthfulness of God to the point of complete reliance upon His ability in your life through Jesus Christ our Lord.

Faith declares: "I trust God even when I do not trust myself. I believe God even when I cannot believe in my own resources." You never base the outcome of your current situation on what you do or do not have. Your outcome is supernatural because the God who called you to purpose is supernatural.

Living Sacrifice and Transformation

Romans 12:1–2 reminds us: "Present your bodies a living sacrifice, holy, acceptable unto God, which is your reasonable service. And be not conformed to this world: but be transformed by the renewing of your mind."

To live under God's perceptual stimuli, you must always be ready to present your body as a living sacrifice. Now, let us understand this truth. There is no blessing in clinging to comfort or safety. Faith rarely grows in the comfort zone. Faith thrives when you are willing to step out of the boat while others remain behind.

The word present means "to stand beside." It is the posture of a servant standing beside his master, ready to do whatever is required. Presenting yourself to God means living with an attitude of readiness—alert, watchful, and surrendered.

But readiness always requires transformation. Transformation means change. It demands a willingness to allow God to re-shape the condition of your heart, the nature of your thinking, and even remove aspects of your character that may hinder what He has ahead. More often than not, this requires overcoming the fear of change and the weight of additional responsibility.

Yet, take courage: God never calls you to change without promising to strengthen you for the journey. The "new" that awaits you is greater than the "old" you leave behind. The latter will always be greater than the former when God is in it.

Renewing the Mind

Operating under perceptual stimuli means renewing your mind. Renewal means a renovation, a complete overhaul in your process of thinking. God calls you to see life in a new and improved way. This requires breaking away from the conventional, the predictable, and the stale.

Sometimes God even calls you to break the rules—yes, even religious rules. Why? Because many of those rules are built on the limitations of human perception rather than the expansiveness of God's revelation. Jesus Himself was accused of being a rule-breaker. He healed on the Sabbath, touched the untouchable, dined with sinners, and taught with authority that offended the religious elite. His methods were unconventional, yet His mission was unstoppable.

True transformation of the mind will challenge your intellect and stretch your understanding. Imagine being Noah, building a massive ark when no one had ever seen rain fall from the sky. To the world, Noah looked foolish, but he was responding to divine stimuli—a sacred signal from Heaven. Faith allowed him to perceive what others could not imagine.

Faith and Perception

Faith is not blind; it is visionary. It sees beyond what is and perceives what will be. Hebrews 11:3 says, "Through faith we understand that the worlds were framed by the word of God." Faith gives understanding—an ability to perceive, comprehend, and interpret what God is doing.

To perceive God is to move beyond natural observation into spiritual comprehension. This is why Hebrews 11:6 is so vital. God is not asking us merely to believe in His existence. He is inviting us to believe in His nearness, His activity, and His rewarding nature. He delights to bless those who seek Him diligently.

The Greek word for "rewarder" here is misthos, meaning "one who pays wages." God is saying, "I will not let your faithfulness go unrewarded. I see your pursuit, I hear your prayers, I honor your trust."

Faith on Trial

Of course, faith is not proven in easy seasons. It is tested in impossible places. James 1:3 tells us, "The trying of your faith produces patience." The word "trying" means a testing for trustworthiness. God allows trials not to break us but to build us.

The transliteration of "knowing" in this verse is ginosko—to know by experience, to perceive in such a way that you can speak what you have understood from God. True faith produces experiential knowledge. It is one thing to hear a sermon about God's faithfulness. It is another to walk through a valley and proclaim, "The Lord is my Shepherd, I shall not want!"

Even Abraham, the father of faith, experienced this. Romans 4:1 asks, "What shall we say then that Abraham our father, as pertaining to the flesh, hath found?" The word "found" here refers to perceiving something so deeply that it changes what you see. Abraham perceived the promises of God until his vision was transformed. Though his body was old and Sarah's womb was barren, he perceived through faith what others could only dismiss.

Incredible Faith for Incredible Outcomes

This is the essence of a life full of incredible outcomes. Your "incredible faith" will always be challenged by "incredible circumstances." But the greater the test, the greater the testimony. The greater the trial, the greater the triumph.

Every incredible outcome begins with the courage to believe beyond what you see. It begins with perceiving that God is able. It begins with stepping out of the comfort zone, renewing your mind, and allowing God's Spirit to lead you into the unknown.

When your faith is tried, let patience have its perfect work. When your back is against the wall, let your trust in God's Word anchor you. For every test of trustworthiness prepares you for the release of greater promises.

Reflection and Application

1. Faith Check: What areas of your life have you been measuring by your own ability instead of God's?

2. Sacrifice Test: Where is God calling you to step out of the comfort zone?

3. Renewal Practice: How can you begin intentionally renewing your mind daily?

4. Perception Shift: What situation requires you to look not at what is, but at what God has spoken?

Prayer:

Lord, grant me the faith to perceive what You are doing. Teach me to trust You beyond what I can see. Transform my mind, renovate my thinking, and prepare me for the incredible outcomes You have destined for me. I yield to Your Spirit, I trust Your voice, and I step into Your promises with confidence. In Jesus 'name, Amen.

~ 2 ~

CREATED IN HIS IMAGE

"So God created man in His own image, in the image of God He created him; male and female He created them." – Genesis 1:27

The Glory of Our Design

To experience the awesome position that God has in store for us, we must know a foundational truth: we are created to resemble God. Knowing this reshapes how we view ourselves, others, and the world. When we realize that we bear His image, we recognize that He made us to communicate clearly with Him and represent Him in the earth.

Just as children are born with the ability to communicate with their parents, we were created with the capacity to commune with our Heavenly Father. Genesis 1:27 makes this clear: "So God created man in His own image, in the image of God He created him; male and female He created them."

When God determined to create humanity, He designed us to be different from everything else in creation. The animals were formed, the plants were spoken into existence, the stars were set in place—but man and woman were uniquely crafted in God's similitude. With this comes a mission: not only to walk in fellowship with Him, but also to exercise dominion and fulfill divine purpose on the earth.

Characteristics of God in Humanity

To be created in the image of God means we carry His characteristics. These are not just abstract qualities but functional attributes that equip us to live in partnership with Him. Among the greatest of these characteristics is creativity. God is a Creator, and therefore we, as His children, are creators.

This does not mean we create from nothing as He did in the beginning, but that we are designed to bring order, innovation, and beauty into a world that is often marked by chaos. We were created to replace darkness with light, emptiness with abundance, and despair with hope.

Jeremiah 29:11 reassures us of this divine intent: "For I know the thoughts that I think toward you, saith the LORD, thoughts of peace, and not of evil, to give you an expected end." God's purpose in creating us in His image was not haphazard. He had an "expected end"—a destiny of peace, fruitfulness, and fulfillment.

The Breath of God in Us

Genesis 2:7 brings us into the intimacy of God's design: "And the LORD God formed man of the dust of the ground, and breathed into his nostrils the breath of life; and man became a living soul."

Before God breathed, man was dust—valuable but lifeless, formed but functionless. It was the neshamah—the divine breath, the infusion of God's own inspiration and intellect—that animated us. At that moment, humanity became more than creation; we became carriers of the Creator.

This truth reveals why life apart from God feels empty. Without the breath of God active in us, we are reduced to dust-level living: bound by limitations, subject to earthly elements, and confined to natural outcomes. But with the breath of God, we are awakened to supernatural possibilities. We live no longer as mere dust, but as vessels of divine inspiration.

Dominion and Authority

Being created in God's image is not only about relationship; it is also about responsibility. Genesis 1:28 outlines this: "And God blessed them, and God said unto them, Be fruitful, and multiply, and replenish the earth, and subdue it: and have dominion..."

Notice the progression:

1. Be fruitful – produce.
2. Multiply – reproduce.
3. Replenish – restore.
4. Subdue – conquer.
5. Have dominion – rule.

These are not casual suggestions; they are divine mandates. To be in His image means to partner with Him in exercising stewardship over the earth. Nothing in creation was given such a mandate. Animals reproduce, plants yield, but only humanity was commanded to rule, subdue, and extend God's order into the earth.

This authority is covenantal. When David confronted Goliath, he asked, "Who is this uncircumcised Philistine that he should defy the armies of the living God?" (1 Samuel 17:26). David understood that covenant with God meant authority over anything outside of that covenant. To be in God's image is to walk in the confidence that nothing in this realm—no giant, no system, no principality—has the right to dominate us.

Ambassadors of God

The Hebrew word for "image" is tselem, meaning "representative figure." We are God's ambassadors in the earth, bearing His likeness to demonstrate His power and presence. This is echoed in

2 Corinthians 5:20: "Now then we are ambassadors for Christ, as though God did beseech you by us."

To be an ambassador is to represent the will, the authority, and the culture of the Kingdom from which you are sent. As image-bearers, we do not reflect the brokenness of the world; we reflect the glory of God. This is why Paul urges us to "take every thought captive to make it obedient to Christ" (2 Corinthians 10:5). We were created to subdue every thought, every system, every lie that sets itself against the knowledge of God.

Thinking Like God

When God breathed into man the neshamah—divine inspiration—He imparted not only life but intellect. This was not ordinary intellect but the capacity to think with God's perspective. Isaiah 55:9 declares, "For as the heavens are higher than the earth, so are my ways higher than your ways, and my thoughts than your thoughts."

Yet, because of Christ, we are invited into those higher thoughts. 1 Corinthians 2:16 reminds us: "But we have the mind of Christ." To walk in His image is to walk with access to His mind, His discernment, and His wisdom. This is the essence of perceptual stimuli—seeing what He sees, hearing what He hears, and discerning what He reveals.

Living in the Fullness of His Image

Being created in His image means that lack is not our destiny. Philippians 4:19 assures us: "But my God shall supply all your need according to His riches in glory by Christ Jesus." God's provision is a natural outflow of His nature, and because we are in His image, His abundance is accessible to us.

But God doesn't stop with needs. Psalm 37:4 declares: "Delight yourself also in the Lord, and He shall give you the desires of your heart." Our identity in His image positions us not only to survive but to thrive, not only to endure but to enjoy the abundant life Christ promised in John 10:10.

This truth dismantles lies of unworthiness, shame, and lack. To be created in God's image is to live with dignity, authority, and destiny.

Reflection and Application

1.   Identity: In what ways have you underestimated the truth that you are created in God's image?
2.   Dominion: What situations in your life are you allowing to dominate you that you should instead subdue?
3.   Creativity: Where can you bring light, order, or beauty into dark or chaotic places?
4.   Breath of God: How can you become more intentional in living by the Spirit's inspiration rather than earthly limitations?

Prayer:

Father, thank You for creating me in Your image. Breathe afresh into me today. Remind me that I carry Your likeness, Your authority, and Your creativity. Teach me to walk in dominion, to reflect Your glory, and to live as an ambassador of Your Kingdom. Let my life reveal the fullness of being made in Your image. In Jesus' name, Amen.

~ 3 ~

YOU ARE A SUPERNATURAL WINNER

"For whom He foreknew, He also predestined to be conformed to the image of His Son, that He might be the firstborn among many brethren." – Romans 8:29

Foreknown and Predestined

In Romans 8:29 we find the word foreknow in the King James Version of the Bible. In the context in which the word is used, it suggests that to live a life of predestination, one must first have been foreknown by God. The Greek transliteration of this word is proginosko. It means not only that God knew everything about you before you were born, but that He also ordained you before you were known by anyone in this earth.

This means God has already established your ability to succeed and become what He designed you to be. Your victory is not an afterthought; it is a divine decree. It is ordained in the spiritual realm, and it is your responsibility to walk into what has already been spoken over your life.

This is why being able to perceive what God is doing is so important. Once you identify with God and His will for your life in this way, you realize what it truly means to be "made to win."

God's Sovereign Knowledge

God knows what is coming before it comes. He knows your heart, your love for Him, your struggles, and your victories. He knows the plans He formed for you before you took your first breath. Because He knows what He created you to be—and because He holds all power in His hands—He causes all things to work together for your good (Romans 8:28).

The question is: Do we know it? Can we perceive what He is doing? The Greek word for know here is closely related to our English word "prognosis"—a prediction about how something will develop. God's prognosis for your life is victory. He has already written your outcome in His book, and the ending is always triumphant.

The Value of Small Beginnings

Being made to win does not mean everything begins in a grand way. Neither does it mean that you will be free from challenges. In fact, God often uses small beginnings and obstacles to develop your character. These moments prepare you to handle greater victories at each level of success.

Zechariah 4:10 says, "Do not despise these small beginnings, for the Lord rejoices to see the work begin." Every giant-killer once fought lions and bears. Every victor has learned to endure trials that forged their strength. Your journey may not start glamorous, but it is glorious because it is God-ordained.

When you understand that you were made to win, you stop obsessing over the challenges and begin focusing on the journey. You realize that every obstacle is not a setback but a setup for growth and greater glory.

The Power of Knowing

This is why the devil is always after what you know. The moment you become aware of who you are in Christ Jesus, anything becomes possible. The enemy cannot undo your victory, but he can try to cloud your perception. If he can keep you ignorant of your identity, he can keep you living beneath your inheritance.

But once revelation comes, no lie of the enemy can overpower the truth you have received. As John 8:32 declares, "You shall know the truth, and the truth shall make you free."

Victory Is Your Portion

When you were born again, you received an anointing that pre-limits your struggles. God knows what will break you, and He knows what will make you. He allows trials only to the extent that they refine you without destroying you. He is more committed to you being a winner than you could ever imagine.

2 Corinthians 2:14 declares: "Now thanks be unto God, who always causes us to triumph in Christ." Notice the word always. Triumph is not occasional; it is continual. It is not circumstantial; it is covenantal.

To triumph means to carry victory as your permanent identity. You may experience battles, but your destiny is triumph. Even in seasons when it doesn't appear that you are winning, God is orchestrating victory behind the scenes.

The Blessed Life

Your life is full of hope, which means pleasurable anticipation and expectation of good. Because God is for you, no one can ultimately stand against you (Romans 8:31). Judgmental tongues may rise against you, but the verdict of Heaven is already in your favor.

The Bible uses two main Greek words for "blessed." The first is makarios—supremely happy. The second is eulogeo—to speak well of, to invoke prosperity. God has spoken well over you. His final Word is a benediction of prosperity, declaring that you will live in more than enough.

This blessing delivers you from the cycle of tragedy-to-tragedy living. It positions you to experience life to the full—needs supplied, desires granted, and joy overflowing.

The Protection of the Winner

Heaven's perspective is this: even though people may have earthly grounds to judge you based on failures, mistakes, or guilt, God will not allow condemnation to stand. Romans 8:33–34 reminds us: "Who shall bring a charge against God's elect? It is God who justifies."

As one who chases after the will of God, you are clothed in divine favor. You carry God-quality within you, making you an instrument of His Kingdom purpose. This is why God has placed a hedge of protection around your life. The enemy may plot, but access is restricted. You are hidden in Christ, and every blessing spoken over you is secured.

Access to the Mysteries of God

Ephesians 1:8 says, "Wherein He hath abounded toward us in all wisdom and prudence." The transliteration for prudence is phronēsis, which means superabundance of mental action and insight. As a believer, you have access to divine strategies that defy human logic. This is why people ask, "How do you know what you know?" It is the gift of perceptual stimuli—the ability to perceive what God is about to do.

Paul also writes in 1 Corinthians 2:7, "But we speak the wisdom of God in a mystery, the hidden wisdom which God ordained before the ages for our glory." The word mystery (mystērion) does not mean unknowable; it means hidden until revealed. Through Christ, you have been granted access to hidden wisdom, favor, and insight that silences your enemies and propels you into victory.

Made to Win

John 3:16 reveals God's motivation: "For God so loved the world that He gave His only begotten Son, that whoever believes in Him should not perish but have everlasting life." Everlasting life is not only eternal duration but abundant quality. It is a life marked by quick turnarounds, divine joy, and constant grace.

Galatians 3:29 confirms: "If you belong to Christ, then you are Abraham's seed, and heirs according to the promise." To be Abraham's seed is to walk in divine assurance. The word promise here implies a formal announcement of guaranteed good over your life. This means you are not hoping for favor; you are heir to it.

Reflection and Application

1. What battles are you facing right now that you need to view through the lens of "I am made to win"?
2. In what ways has the enemy tried to attack your knowledge of your identity in Christ?
3. How can you live more consciously aware that triumph is your covenant portion, not just an occasional experience?

Prayer:

Father, thank You that You foreknew me and predestined me for victory. I declare that I am not a victim but a supernatural winner. Cause me to see every obstacle as a step toward triumph. Silence every lie of the enemy and awaken in me the certainty of Your promise. I walk in the blessing, favor, and protection of being Your child. In Jesus 'name, Amen.

PART II – DESTINY & DIVINE ALIGNMENT

~ 4 ~

YOU HAVE A DATE WITH DESTINY

"And we know that all things work together for good to them that love God, to them who are the called according to His purpose." -- Romans 8:28

Awareness of Destiny

God wants you to clearly be aware of how He intends to use your life to bring Him glory, honor, and praise. This awareness separates ordinary living from Kingdom living. It transforms you from someone who stumbles through circumstances into someone who makes life happen under divine guidance.

In Romans 8:28, the word know is transliterated eido, which means to be aware, to perceive, to understand with certainty. God desires that you live with this kind of knowing—that you are not guessing about your destiny but perceiving it with clarity.

This awareness is life-transforming. Your date with destiny is not secured by your perfection but by your perfect decision to love and surrender to God. Every yes you have said to Him has aligned you with the path of His purpose.

Called According to His Purpose

By virtue of reading this book, you have already demonstrated that you want to make your calling and election sure. That puts you in the perfect position—called according to the purpose of God.

The Greek word for purpose (prothesis) refers to "setting forth with intention." It is the same word used to describe the show-bread in the Temple—the Bread of the Presence that remained continually before God. This means your life is a memorial before the Lord, a living testimony that His promises are true. You are like the bread of His presence—your very existence is evidence of His covenant faithfulness.

Romans 8:28–31 shows us that destiny is not accidental. It is a divine design—a series of aligned events strategically placed in your life to guide you to the exact doors God intends to open. Destiny is the divine GPS, recalculating every detour, realigning every setback, ensuring that no matter what happens, the route still leads to His intended destination.

Destiny in the Midst of Difficulty

Your overall life circumstances—including the painful ones—are not random. They are alignment points. This does not mean that every hardship came from God, but it does mean that God redeems and re-purposes even the hardest things for your good.

To identify with your destiny, you must push beyond pain, disappointment, and loss. This is not to minimize the weight of what you've endured but to remind you: it is not the end. The enemy may have meant it for evil, but God is turning it for good (Genesis 50:20).

Your future is cheering you on. Destiny is pulling you forward. Heaven itself anticipates your victory.

Destiny Anchored in Promise

2 Corinthians 1:20 assures us: "For all the promises of God in Him are yea, and in Him Amen, unto the glory of God by us." Every promise God has spoken is guaranteed in Christ. But notice the phrase *in Him*. The promises are not unlocked by striving in our own strength; they are accessed by abiding in Him.

This means that fulfilling destiny is about alignment with His presence. When you walk in Him, you walk into promises that are already waiting at certain levels of your journey. They do not come down to you; you must grow up into them.

This is why Paul declared in Philippians 3:14, "I press toward the mark for the prize of the high calling of God in Christ Jesus." To press means to pursue with passion and determination, to strain forward with relentless focus. Pressing is not passive—it is aggressive pursuit. It is throwing yourself fully into God's purpose without regard for safety or convenience.

The Power of God's "Yes"

When God says His promises are "yes" in Him, it is more than affirmation. The Greek word *nai* used here means a strong, absolute affirmation. Heaven's yes is not like man's yes—it cannot be revoked, it cannot be diluted, it cannot be reversed.

Numbers 23:19 declares, "God is not a man, that He should lie; neither the son of man, that He should repent: hath He said, and shall He not do it?" God's yes over your life is settled. Your responsibility is to rise and pursue until you live out what He has spoken.

A Life That Influences Others

Living in destiny means living exposed. Just as the showbread was set before God, your life is set before both Heaven and Earth.

You are a testimony on display, proof of His covenant-keeping power.

This is why your life influences others more than you realize. Destiny is not private—it provokes action in others, ignites revival, and releases the anointing of God into atmospheres. When you walk in destiny, chains break, oppression lifts, and freedom is released—not just for you, but for everyone connected to you.

Romans 8:31 asks: "If God be for us, who can be against us?" The answer is obvious: no one. God's yes silences every "no" of man. God's favor outweighs every opposition. And Romans 8:32 goes further: "He that spared not His own Son, but delivered Him up for us all, how shall He not with Him also freely give us all things?"

Did you catch that? God has already proven His willingness to give you everything by giving you His Son. Therefore, nothing needed for your destiny will be withheld. Your date with destiny has been set; your rendezvous is certain.

Pressing Into Your Next Level

Your role is to press—reach forth, stretch forth, and move toward your next level. This requires faith, perseverance, and obedience. It requires refusing to settle for where you are when you know God has more. It means living with holy discontent, always stretching toward greater alignment with His purpose.

Destiny requires pursuit. It requires passion. It requires the refusal to quit when obstacles rise. And it requires confidence that the One who called you is faithful to bring you into completion (Philippians 1:6).

Reflection and Application

1. What past pain or disappointment do you need to reframe as part of your alignment toward destiny?

2. What promises has God spoken over your life that you must "press" toward in this season?
3. How can your life become a greater testimony of God's covenant-keeping power to those around you?

Prayer:

Father, thank You for calling me according to Your purpose. Thank You that my destiny is secure in You and that every promise is "yes and amen" in Christ. Strengthen me to press toward the mark with passion and perseverance. Open my eyes to see destiny unfolding in my daily steps, and give me boldness to live as a testimony of Your covenant faithfulness. I receive my date with destiny, and I step into my next level with confidence in Jesus 'name, Amen.

~ 5 ~

EXPERIENCE YOUR NEXT LEVEL

"And it shall come to pass, if thou shalt hearken diligently unto the voice of the LORD thy God, to observe and to do all his commandments which I command thee this day, that the LORD thy God will set thee on high above all nations of the earth."
– Deuteronomy 28:1

Hearing the Voice of God

As we begin to live a life of perceptual stimuli, we must be able to hearken diligently to the voice of God. Deuteronomy 28:1 gives us this condition for elevation: if we hearken diligently, He will set us on high.

The Hebrew word for hearken is shama, meaning "to hear intelligently." This is not casual listening; it is hearing with attention, comprehension, and intent to obey. Hearing God requires tuning in to the fine details of His instructions, because His words often carry eternal implications.

The word diligently is described by three expressions: wholly, speedily, and vehemently. Each of these carries weight for those who desire to live on the "next level" with God.

Hearing Wholly

First, God expects us to respond wholly. This means with single-minded devotion. Our ears must be tuned to His agenda above all else. To hear wholly is to live with focus so sharp that distractions cannot derail you from the assignment God has given.

Think of Samuel as a boy in the temple. When God called, "Samuel! Samuel!" (1 Samuel 3), Samuel learned to reply, "Speak, Lord, for Your servant hears." That posture—total attention to God's voice—positioned him to become a prophet who carried weight in Israel.

Hearing wholly means setting aside competing voices—our fears, culture's demands, even our own ambitions—to obey the Lord's command without compromise.

Hearing with Urgency

Second, to hear diligently is to hear with urgency. Sometimes God speaks not about what will happen someday, but about what must happen now.

You shared your testimony of repeatedly seeing "911," which God revealed not as an emergency but as urgency. In the same way, God often places assignments before us that cannot afford delay. They are time-sensitive Kingdom tasks.

Paul reminds us in Romans 13:11, "Knowing the time, that now it is high time to awake out of sleep: for now is our salvation nearer than when we believed." To delay obedience is to risk missing divine timing. Next-level believers treat God's instructions as urgent and respond without procrastination.

Hearing with Passion

Third, diligence requires passion. The word vehemently means with zeal, fervor, and intensity. God is not looking for half-hearted obedience but burning devotion. Jesus said in Revelation 3:16 that lukewarmness makes Him want to "spew out." Passionate obedience pleases God.

Jeremiah described God's word like "a fire shut up in my bones" (Jeremiah 20:9). When you perceive God's instruction, it ought to burn within you until you move. Your next level is not accessed by casual Christianity but by zealous pursuit of God's will.

Experiencing God in Communion

Your personal prayer life is key. Prayer is not just petition but communion—a two-way conversation with God. It is in prayer that your sensitivity is sharpened and your perception fine-tuned.

Prayer opens you to not only hear His words but also to experience His presence. You feel His power, His glory, His virtue. This communion becomes a fire that comforts and empowers, stirring an awareness of the spiritual realm.

Moses experienced this when he communed with God on Mount Sinai. His face shone so brightly with glory that the people were afraid to look at him (Exodus 34:29). Prayer changes perception. Communion ushers you into the awareness needed to walk in your next level.

Worship as a Next Level Experience

Next-level living requires next-level worship. John 4:24 declares, "God is Spirit: and they that worship Him must worship Him in spirit and in truth." To worship in spirit is to perceive the infinite possibilities of who God is.

When you perceive His greatness, worship shifts. It becomes more than songs and words—it becomes tears of expectation, moments of intimacy, encounters with His overwhelming love. Worship pulls you into the atmosphere of Heaven where breakthrough becomes inevitable.

Isaiah encountered this in Isaiah 6 when he saw the Lord high and lifted up. That vision led him to cry out, "Here am I; send me." Worship reveals destiny, transforms perspective, and thrusts you into divine assignments.

The Revelation of God's Love

When you worship at the next level, you begin to perceive the immensity of God's love. Paul describes this in Romans 8:38–39, declaring he was "persuaded" that nothing could separate us from God's love. The Greek word peitho means "to agree."

Paul's revelation is profound: once you encounter God's love, you must agree with it. You must believe it so strongly that no trial, demon, or failure can convince you otherwise.

This love cannot be divorced, separated, or put asunder. It clings to you through every season. Worship encounters lead you into this awareness, leaving you in awe of a love that surpasses knowledge.

Living in Next-Level Perception

Your next level is not just about elevation in status—it is about elevation in perception. It is living with heightened spiritual awareness, recognizing God's movements even when they defy human understanding.

This is what Paul meant when he said in 2 Corinthians 5:7, "We walk by faith, not by sight." Next-level believers perceive what is not visible, discern what is not obvious, and move in alignment with what the Spirit reveals.

When your perception is stimulated by the Spirit of God, your attitude shifts, your worship deepens, and your faith stabilizes.

You stop being discouraged by what you experience and become encouraged by what you perceive.

Reflection and Application

1. In what areas of life do you need to listen more "wholly"—without distraction or divided focus?
2. What urgent assignment has God placed before you that requires immediate obedience?
3. How can you fuel greater passion and zeal in your pursuit of God's next level for your life?
4. How has worship recently shifted your perspective of God's love?

Prayer:

Lord, thank You for calling me higher. Teach me to hear Your voice wholly, urgently, and passionately. Let my prayer life sharpen my perception, and let my worship become a place of encounter where I am overwhelmed by Your love. Elevate my perception, increase my awareness, and empower me to step into my next level with confidence and faith. In Jesus 'name, Amen.

~ 6 ~

CREATED FOR SO MUCH MORE

"But seek ye first the kingdom of God, and his righteousness; and all these things shall be added unto you." – Matthew 6:33

Seeking the Kingdom First

Take a look at what Jesus says in Matthew 6:33: "But seek ye first the kingdom of God, and His righteousness; and all these things shall be added unto you." The Greek word for seek is zeteo, which means "to worship, to strive after, to endeavor with pursuit." This suggests that seeking God is not passive curiosity; it is active worship expressed in pursuit of His will.

So the real question is: Are you committed to worship God until you clearly know His plan for your life? Are you willing to be so devoted that you become an unstoppable force within the earth?

To seek first the Kingdom is to place God's realm, His agenda, and His priorities above your own. That is why Jesus taught us to pray, "Thy kingdom come. Thy will be done in earth, as it is in heaven" (Matthew 6:10). Our prayer life must reflect this divine alignment—bringing Heaven's realities into Earth's conditions.

Gifts, Talents, and Purpose

People often ask, "How do I know what God has called me to do?" The answer is often found in the gifts and talents He has placed within you. Your unique abilities are not random; they were designed to meet needs in the earth.

When you recognize and accept what God has gifted you to do, you will begin to see how He intends to manifest His Kingdom through you. Your gift is the key to your assignment, and your assignment unlocks your destiny. Proverbs 18:16 says, "A man's gift maketh room for him, and bringeth him before great men."

Laying Aside Hindrances

But there is something that must be laid aside if you are to live for so much more: sin. Hebrews 12:1 urges us to lay aside every weight and the sin that so easily entangles us. The only way to truly lay sin aside is to give it to Jesus.

Romans 10:9 assures us: "If you confess with your mouth the Lord Jesus, and believe in your heart that God raised Him from the dead, you will be saved." Sin does not disqualify you from God's plan; unbelief in His redemptive power does. When you trust His forgiveness, His blood cleanses you, and His Spirit empowers you to run your race.

Philippians 1:6 reminds us to be confident: "He who began a good work in you will complete it until the day of Jesus Christ." God is committed to finishing what He started in your life.

The Promise of Abundant Life

Jesus declared in John 10:10 that one of His primary missions was to bring us into abundant life. This abundant life is not merely survival—it is advantage. It is living with the edge of divine favor and supernatural provision.

When you walk in God's plan, every step is saturated with advantage. Obstacles become opportunities, and setbacks become setups. Abundant life means more than enough—enough for you, and overflow for others.

The Divine Helper

Jesus made provision for this life by promising the Comforter. John 14:16 says, "And I will pray the Father, and He shall give you another Comforter, that He may abide with you forever."

The word Comforter (parakletos) means advocate, intercessor, consoler, and helper. This Divine Paraclete is not temporary. He abides forever, guiding, strengthening, and empowering. The Holy Spirit is the presence of God dwelling within every believer.

Acts 1:8 reinforces this: "But ye shall receive power, after that the Holy Ghost is come upon you: and ye shall be witnesses..." The word power (dynamis) means miraculous ability, strength, and might. When the Spirit fills you, He equips you with supernatural capacity. Imagine if every believer tapped into this dynamis—the earth would be transformed.

The Character of the Spirit

To understand the Spirit, we must know His character. He is holy (hagios)—sacred, pure, consecrated. Therefore, He will never guide you into anything that contradicts the Word of God.

He is Spirit (pneuma)—breath, wind, the life-giving force. Because God is Spirit, the only way to connect with Him is through the Spirit. That is why worship must be in Spirit and in truth (John 4:24). The Holy Spirit awakens us to perceive spiritual realities so that we can discern and fulfill Kingdom assignments.

Baptized and Filled

Acts 1:5 speaks of being baptized with the Holy Ghost. The word baptizo means to be immersed, whelmed, overcome. Spirit baptism results in both inward transformation and outward demonstration.

Acts 2:4 describes believers being filled (pimplemi) with the Holy Spirit, meaning supplied, influenced, and empowered to accomplish. This filling convinces us that God has already equipped us with everything we need to fulfill His purpose.

1 Peter 2:9 calls us a chosen (eklektos) generation, a royal priesthood, a peculiar people. To be chosen is to be favored. To be peculiar means set apart for extraordinary purpose. The Spirit fills us so we can show forth His praises and demonstrate His light in a dark world.

Living Under Grace

Romans 5:1 reminds us that, justified by faith, we have peace with God. This peace introduces us to grace. The Greek word charis means divine influence, favor, and benefit. Grace is not just pardon—it is empowerment. It is living under divine influence where good and perfect gifts continually flow into your life (James 1:17).

Grace lifts you from level to level, from favor to favor. It is the constant reminder that you were created for more than mediocrity. You were created to manifest Heaven's goodness on earth.

Created for More

Joel 2:28 declares that in the last days God would pour out His Spirit, causing sons and daughters to prophesy, young men to see visions, and old men to dream dreams. Your dreams, visions, and prophetic insights are proof that you were created for more.

The Spirit of God is stirring within you, making you aware that your gifts are marketable, your purpose undeniable, and your calling unstoppable. You were born to meet a need in the earth, to solve a problem, to shift an atmosphere.

This is why fear tries to silence you. But 2 Timothy 1:7 declares: "For God has not given us the spirit of fear; but of power, and of love, and of a sound mind." Fear is not your inheritance—power is. Soundness of mind is. Perceptual stimuli is. You have everything you need to walk into your destiny.

Reflection and Application

1.   What gifts or talents has God given you that point to your divine purpose?
2.   What worldly entanglements or distractions do you need to lay aside to live fully for Him?
3.   How can you lean more intentionally on the Holy Spirit as your Comforter, Advocate, and Guide?
4.   In what ways is God calling you to step boldly into your "more" right now?

Prayer:

Father, thank You for creating me for more than I have experienced. Thank You for gifting me, redeeming me, and filling me with Your Spirit. I yield to Your divine influence and embrace the abundant life You promised. Stir within me the courage to release the greatness You placed inside me. May my life manifest Your Kingdom on earth as it is in Heaven. In Jesus 'name, Amen.

PART III – FAVOR, TRANSFER, AND INCREASE

~ 7 ~

YOUR FAVOR IS DIVINE

"For thou, LORD, wilt bless the righteous; with favor wilt thou compass him as with a shield." — Psalm 5:12

The Shield That Surrounds You

In Psalms 5:12 the word of God says "For thou, LORD, wilt bless the righteous; with favor wilt thou compass him as with a shield". The two words "Divine" and "Favor" describe your life when your perception is stimulated by the Holy Ghost. Divine means that it is emanating from God and resulting from His Divine Providence. The transliteration of "Favor" is (Rason), which means an advantage given to you that will be to your benefit. As a regenerated believer you are protected or compassed with favor. This means that God encircles you with favor to protect you. Sometimes this even includes being protected from yourself.

God's favor is not a thin mist; it is a shield—thick, encompassing, and strategically positioned to intercept what was meant to wound you. Visualize it: front, back, left, right, above, beneath—favor is your circumference. Even when you can't explain how the arrow missed, or why the timing worked out "just so," it is the encircling shield of favor at work. Favor is not random; it is covenantal. It accompanies the righteous because righteousness aligns you with the King whose presence releases it.

God is determined to demonstrate his Glory in your life, so that his power can be demonstrated. This is why Psalms 30:5 says "For his anger endures but a moment; in his favor is life: weeping may endure for a night, but joy cometh in the morning". The word used for "life" listed above is "Hay", which means to revive, to keep alive, or give promise. It also means to nourish up and repair. This means that God is committed to fix you and your situation. Hear him, because he is leading you to repair. Perceive that he is restoring your soul and repairing your breach. He can put you and what you are dealing with back together better than it ever was before. Of course you do not deserve it and yes you were the cause of it, but that is what makes it divine. It begins with God and it is his power that completes the process.

In His favor is life. Not mere survival, but revival—renewal that nourishes and repairs. Divine favor doesn't just spare you; it restores you. It is the spiritual "yes" that overrules the enemy's "no," the heavenly verdict that cancels the earthly accusation. Grace pours in where guilt once sat, and the outcome testifies: "This was the Lord's doing; it is marvelous in our eyes." (Psalm 118:23)

Standing Watch at the Doors of Favor

Take a look at Proverbs 8:32-36. It begins by imploring us to Hearken. We should be alert and on the lookout for the next favor moment. He says that we should wait at the posts of his doors. This demonstrates to us that God always has an opening or entrance way for us that leads to favor. When you are walking in perceptual stimuli, you are constantly having secret sessions with God.

Waiting at Wisdom's doorposts is postured expectancy. You are not begging for scraps—you are positioning for strategy. Favor loves obedience; it accompanies those who "hearken." You don't chase random opportunities; you stand where God posts you, watch at the threshold He indicates, and walk through the door He opens (Revelation 3:8). Perceptual stimuli keeps you alert—awake to subtle nudges, attentive to divine timings, poised for divine entrances.

Look at Psalms 25:14 "The secret of the LORD is with them that fear him; and he will shew them his covenant". The word used here for "Secret" is "Sode" meaning an intimate session with God where you receive consultation, during what is declared a secret assembly.

He invites you to confidential briefings. In the "sode" of the Lord, He discloses the blueprint behind the blessing—the covenant logic of favor. There, He not only announces outcomes; He trains your perception so you can recognize favor's fingerprints in motion.

Salvation: The Gateway Into Divine Favor

Being born again is the most wonderful decision that you have ever made and if you are reading this book and have never surrendered your life to Christ; today is your day. In the book of Romans 10:9 it says "That if thou shalt confess with thy mouth the Lord Jesus, and shalt believe in thine heart that God hath raised him from the dead, thou shalt be saved". First and foremost we are saved from the penalty of our sins. All of us have committed them at some point in life, which means that we deserved to die and go to hell. But God!!! He forgives us and cleanses us from all unrighteousness. Additionally he does so much more. He not only saves us, but he gives us this supernatural power and ability to transform our lives and achieve true life, success, joy, and peace.

Favor is not earned; it is inherited in Christ. Salvation moves you from judgment to justification, from striving to standing, from scarcity to sonship. You are not outside peeking in; you are family, seated with Christ (Ephesians 2:6), a participant in covenant promises that carry favor by design.

Born of God — Born to Overcome

In 1st John 5:4 the word of God says "For whatsoever is born of God overcometh the world: and this is the victory that overcometh the world, even our faith". When you are regenerated by the Holy Spirit of Promise, you are instantly translated into the league of "Overcomers". No matter what obstacle you may face, or the dilemmas lurking around the next corner of your life. You have Divine Favor that causes things to eventually maneuver to for your advantage. Keep standing, keep pushing, keep praying, keep believing, keep your measure of faith alive, because your turn around is nigh you. Just position yourself to "Perceive" what God is doing on your behalf.

There is nothing fair or understandable to most about the favor that you possess. Though it may not be fair, it is most certainly "Just". It is just, because it is divine. No one can deny your outcome and no one can stop your forward motion. God in you is greater than anything in this world. Can you feel that stirring something on the inside of who you are?

Because you invoke "Perceptual Stimulation" you are more than a conqueror. Because of what Jesus has done for you, and because you have made him Lord of your life, you can hear his voice. Not following another, because you can perceive his divine presence in your life. His divine favor comforts you in every storm, directs you in every dark place, protects you during each and every attack. You may even see thousands fall at your side, but look at you. You are still standing!!! Why? Because your Favor is Divine!!!

The transliterated word used for "overcometh" is (Nikao), which means to subdue, conquer, overcome, prevail, and get the victory. It infers that you are taken on a conquest that becomes your means of success and victory. It is where your favor is demonstrated and revealed.

Favor doesn't remove every battle; it reframes every battle. You fight from victory, not for it. Nikao is your assignment and your assurance—favor equips you to subdue what once subdued you. Through each confrontation, God showcases His triumph in you (2 Corinthians 2:14).

Unsearchable Riches and the Prosperity of the Soul

In the book of Ephesians the third chapter and the eighth verse the Apostle Paul writes about the "unsearchable riches of Christ". There is so much that God has to offer you that it literally is unsearchable. Now you must understand that context in which this is intended, because it is different from what most have come to understand. The transliteration implies that what God is bestowing to you cannot be tracked out or that it is untraceable, and beyond finding out. In other words, so much of your success is going to baffle the Nay Sayers and doubters that you encounter. Now these riches that the Apostle Paul speak of are more than eternal security, but also include Wealth as Fullness, Money, Possessions or Abundance, and Valuable Bestowment. Take a look for yourself at the transliteration which is "Ploutos".

Your favor will inevitably lead you to prosperity. If you are being led by perceptual stimuli, you have already insured that your soul is prospering and if your soul is prospering, then your whole life should be prosperous.

This is not prosperity detached from purpose; it is ploutos aligned with assignment. The riches are "unsearchable"—not because they are imaginary, but because they are sourced in Christ's inexhaustible fullness (Colossians 2:9–10). Favor funds the mission. Expect provision that matches your calling, not your comfort zone.

Enlightened to See and Stirred to Act

In the next verse Paul speaks of the ability to see. Don't miss this!!! To "see" means to enlighten, bring to, and make to see. This is showing us that God is reaching into our intellect so that the power of the faculty of our minds can be enlightened. This is God stirring your perception until you can apprehend his movement in the earth realm by means of stimulating your senses. Simultaneously this stimulation is something that is inciting you to action. You have this confidence in this motivation to act because you having previously experienced it in the spiritual realm that was so real that it was as if it were something actually being encountered for the first time.

Favor opens eyes before it opens doors. Illumination precedes advancement. When the Spirit enlightens the "eyes of your understanding" (Ephesians 1:18), you begin to recognize opportunities that were always there. Discernment converts revelation into motion—you move because you've seen.

God is waiting to fill you with all of his fullness, meaning he wants to satisfy your desires, because you have delighted yourself in him. He is more than ready to execute purpose in your life until you see the full manifestation of his perfect plan in you. Your favor is to be displayed to an unusual degree that leaves those around you speechless. You have an expected end that is much like a cord as an attachment, or you are tied to your destiny, which should leave you full of expectation.

Let this settle in your spirit: you are tethered to triumph. The "expected end" (Jeremiah 29:11) is not a vague hope; it is a covenant cord pulling you toward fulfillment. Favor is the gentle but unbreakable draw of God's purpose, assuring that what He started, He will finish.

Practicing Favor—Daily Applications

1. Stand at the Doorposts: Start your day asking, "Lord, where is Your open door today?" Wait at His thresholds with expectation.
2. Schedule Your "Sode": Build daily "secret sessions" with God—quiet, uninterrupted counsel where He shares strategy.
3. Agree With Grace: When condemnation whispers, answer with covenant. Declare Psalm 30:5 and Romans 8:1 over your life.
4. Move on Illumination: When the Spirit enlightens something (a person to call, a task to complete, a step to take), act quickly—favor loves prompt obedience.
5. Testify as You Go: Record "favor moments" each week. Your testimony trains your perception to recognize the shield that surrounds you.

Reflection & Prayer

Reflection Questions

- Where have you recently noticed God's favor shielding you—perhaps protecting you from a decision or redirecting your steps?
- Which "doorposts" is the Lord asking you to watch this week? What will waiting look like in practice?
- In what area do you need to exchange self-condemnation for God's repairing favor (Psalm 30:5)?
- How can you steward "ploutos" (resources, relationships, opportunities) to serve your assignment rather than your comfort?

Prayer

Father, thank You for surrounding me with favor as a shield. Enlighten the eyes of my understanding to recognize Your openings and obey Your instructions. Repair what is broken, revive what has faded, and restore what was stolen. Let unsearchable riches align with my assignment, and let my life publicly display Your covenant faithfulness. I agree with Your love, I stand in Your righteousness, and I walk in divine favor—today and always. In Jesus 'name, Amen.

~ 8 ~

EXPERIENCING THE BLESSING TRANSFER

"Therefore thy gates shall be open continually; they shall not be shut day nor night; that men may bring unto thee the forces of the Gentiles, and that their kings may be brought." — Isaiah 60:11

Understanding the Transfer

As you live a life of perceptual stimuli, God will transfer things into your life that were either in the hands of the wicked or in the hands of unfaithful and unbelieving servants. The word transfer means to cause a change of ownership from one to another.

Isaiah, whose very name means "God is Salvation," prophesied in Isaiah 60:11, "Therefore thy gates shall be open continually; they shall not be shut day nor night; that men may bring unto thee the forces of the Gentiles, and that their kings may be brought." The word forces (hayil) speaks of means, resources, wealth, company, goods, riches, and substance. In other words, God intends for the treasures of the nations to be transferred into the hands of His covenant people.

Divine transference is not just about resources changing hands—it is about stewardship changing alignment. God entrusts resources to those who will advance His Kingdom.

The Reality of Opposition

Whenever God orchestrates a transfer, it creates a stirring in the spiritual realm that often provokes enemies. Consider Saul's jealousy toward David. When favor shifted and David's name was sung more than Saul's (1 Samuel 18:7), Saul hurled spears in envy. Similarly, when Joseph was promoted in Egypt, his brothers struggled to accept the new reality of his position.

Do not be surprised when blessing transfer attracts criticism, jealousy, or even sabotage attempts. What once belonged to another but now belongs to you will be contested—but it cannot be stopped.

Ecclesiastes and the Wealth of the Wicked

Ecclesiastes 2:26 declares, "For God giveth to a man that is good in his sight wisdom, and knowledge, and joy: but to the sinner he giveth travail, to gather and to heap up, that he may give to him that is good before God. This also is vanity and vexation of spirit."

This scripture paints a picture of divine redistribution. God allows the wicked to labor, gather, and store—but ultimately, the wealth they accumulate is transferred to those who walk upright before Him. This is not random; it is covenant justice.

Power to Get Wealth

Deuteronomy 8:18 reinforces this principle: "But thou shalt remember the LORD thy God: for it is he that giveth thee power to get wealth, that he may establish his covenant which he sware unto thy fathers, as it is this day."

The word power here means capacity, ability, and strength. Wealth creation is not simply about human skill—it is embedded into your spiritual DNA as a Kingdom citizen. You don't just have the ability to acquire wealth; you are empowered by covenant identity to walk in supernatural provision.

This transfer is not just about survival. It is about establishing covenant in the earth. Wealth and resources are tools for Kingdom expansion.

Delivered into Marvelous Light

Colossians 1:13 says that God has delivered us from the power of darkness and translated us into the Kingdom of His dear Son. This transfer is more than freedom from sin; it is freedom from insufficiency, fear, and lack. God's light is full of revelation that shifts us from barely enough into more than enough.

Just as rivers flowed into Eden, watering and multiplying its fruitfulness (Genesis 2:10–14), God is opening floodgates of possibility and potential in your life. His blessing transfer is designed to expand your territory and make you a distribution center for His goodness.

Swift and Surprising

When God moves, it is often swift and surprising. Blessing transfer happens suddenly, even when you feel least prepared. Think of Israel leaving Egypt. After 400 years of slavery, in one night, the wealth of Egypt was transferred into their hands (Exodus 12:35–36). They did not have to fight for it—they simply obeyed, perceived the moment, and received the transfer.

When it happens, it may catch others by surprise, but it will not surprise you—because you have been perceiving it in your spirit long before it manifests. Your faith is the title deed (Hebrews 11:1).

Faith as the Bidding

You may feel impatient as you wait for promises to manifest. But remember: every divine promise is already "Yes and Amen" in Christ (2 Corinthians 1:20). The Holy Spirit would not alert you if it were not coming.

Think of Peter on the water. He did not simply step out of the boat on assumption. He said, "Lord, if it be thou, bid me come unto thee on the water." (Matthew 14:28) Peter understood that faith is not self-initiated; it is response-initiated. Faith responds to the bidding of God.

When God bids you, He also anoints you to walk where others sink, to stand where others fall, and to thrive where others drown. Blessing transfer requires obedient faith to step when the bidding comes.

Biblical Patterns of Transfer

- Abraham and Egypt (Genesis 12:16): Pharaoh gave Abraham sheep, oxen, and wealth, even when the circumstances seemed against him.
- Israel and the Promised Land (Joshua 24:13): God gave them cities they did not build and vineyards they did not plant.
- Esther and Haman's Estate (Esther 8:1–2): The estate of the enemy was transferred to Esther and Mordecai.
- Joseph in Egypt (Genesis 41:41–44): Joseph moved from prisoner to governor, entrusted with resources to save nations.

In each case, the transfer was not random. It was purposeful, covenantal, and time-sensitive.

Preparing for Your Transfer

1. Stay Positioned at Open Gates: Keep your heart expectant, like those who wait at Wisdom's doors (Proverbs 8:34).
2. Walk in Obedience: Transfer is for those who are aligned with God's covenant, not those chasing shortcuts.
3. Guard Against Envy: Do not despise the success of others. Celebrate their blessing while perceiving your own coming transfer.
4. Steward Faithfully: When resources shift to you, manage them with integrity. Transfer is about stewardship, not just acquisition.

Reflection and Application

- What resources, opportunities, or relationships might God be preparing to transfer into your life?
- How can you position yourself to hear His bidding clearly?
- Where do you sense impatience that needs to be surrendered in trust?

Prayer:

Father, thank You that You are the God of transfer. Thank You for moving resources, opportunities, and blessings into the hands of Your covenant people. Position my heart to perceive Your bidding, to obey without hesitation, and to steward faithfully what You entrust to me. I declare that the gates are open, the promises are yes, and my inheritance is secure in Christ. In Jesus 'name, Amen.

PART IV – VICTORY OVER OPPOSITION

~ 9 ~

EXPERIENCING THE BLESSING TRANSFER

"Behold, I give unto you power... over all the power of the enemy: and nothing shall by any means hurt you." — Luke 10:19

It has always been and will always be the plan of God for His human creation to be His Image on earth. You must realize that someone has always and will always have a major problem with this. Take a look at Isaiah 14:12 which says "How art thou fallen from heaven, O Lucifer, son of the morning! how art thou cut down to the ground, which didst weaken the nations"! You have very real enemies that do not like your position on earth, in fact they are completely jealous of you. The ring leader of this hatred and jealousy is the devil himself. He does not like the position that you possess. This why Isaiah 14:13 tells the account of his failure to submit, and rebel. It says "For thou hast said in thine heart, I will ascend into heaven, I will exalt my throne above the stars of God: I will sit also upon the mount of the congregation, in the sides of the north": Your priestly position is a magnanimous threat to the areas of darkness, which clearly explains why you are being attacked the way that you are. But you must never forget that the war has already been won, you simply must strategically position yourself to get the special instructions that you have been awaiting to be victorious in every battle. Consider this; in Psalms 37:23 the scripture relays "The steps of a good man are ordered by the

Lord: and he delighteth in his way". The transliteration for ordered is "kuwn" which means that God has ordained, directed, set
up or steps to prosperity. He has designed our lives to go from
one level of success and good fortune to another. You do not need
to fear because the end has been known from the beginning. This
is why you must focus on your task no matter what the struggle
looks like. The book of Isaiah 14:15 it lets us know that the war
is already won. "Yet thou shalt be brought down to hell, to the
sides of the pit". Consider this; the Hebrew transliteration of the
word Hell is (showl) which means the world of the dead and the
transliteration of the word pit is (bowr), which means a hole used
for prison. The devil does not have the authority to operate in the
earth realm with power. The Bible teaches us that Jesus took every
ability that satan had to release the spirit of failure and captivity
(Ephesians 4:8). He has no authority or power to have victory over
your life.

The devil is not happy about us being made in the image of
God, because that is what he wanted and even more than that he
wanted to be God. This caused his fall along with every other an-
gel that followed him. The devil wanted everything and was con-
vinced that he could be a better god than our Father in heaven. So
to think that God would create man to be like himself and to have
the ability to subdue and have dominion created great disdain toward the existence of humanity (Genesis 1:26 & Genesis 3:14-15) .

In Romans 8:29 we see these words, " For whom he did foreknow, he also did predestinate to be conformed to the image of his
Son, that he might be the firstborn among many brethren". The
concept of God knowing us before we were born is a very eye opening idea. He knew what our passions would be, what kind of weak-
nesses we would have, and most of all what it would take for us to
achieve the ultimate success that he planned for our lives. We see
a perfect example of this in Job 1:10-12, when the devil addressed
that God had placed a hedge of protection around Job, and even

when God gave the devil permission to attack Job in order to discredit him, he could not take Job's life. God knows our character, because he gave it to us and He knows what we can handle. We must trust this part of God, so that even when we are in difficult situation that try our faith, we must trust that He has a greater awareness of who we are and what our limitations may be than we do of ourselves. The Greek transliteration of the word "Predestinate" is proorizo. Interestingly it means to limit in advance. The ultimate goal is for us to do greater works within this earth operating as a type of Christ in the earth, however for this to be accomplished we could not be overcome by temptation and distractions. We have to remain focused on what we have been commissioned to fulfill. God has made it so that if we are in tune with Him we can identify the limits that He has placed within our lives in advance. We can recognize that when there are things that our flesh would love to be a part of or when we simply do not fit in with others even though we try with everything within us, we inevitably have to concede and surrender to it not being a part of the plan for our lives. These limits are to keep us on track and taking the most direct route to our personal place of promise. Think about the times that a door of opportunity has been shut on you, or something that you wanted with everything within you and did not receive. All the while you were praying to God to use you or to only allow those things into your life that He has in store for you. Our flesh and the carnal desires that go with it become a major distraction to fulfilling Kingdom Destiny. James says it best in Ja. 1:14 "But every man is tempted, when he is drawn away of his own lust, and enticed". God wants us to get to a place that we can identify the carnal distractions. They usually are things that we have a tendency to like or are easily drawn to, therefore they can easily take us off course. This is not to say that God will not allow you to experience or even enjoy the things that you are drawn to if they are healthy for you and not damaging to you spiritually. However sometimes you can miss your God given chance by being drawn to a good thing at the wrong time. We have to be able to discern the seasons before us so that we are not lulled into a good thing at a bad time or even fooled to think that something that appears bad is not a move of God. In Romans 8:28 we find these encouraging words "And we know that all things work together for good to them that love God, to them who are the called according to his purpose". This literally means that everything, which includes closed doors, abandonment, and pain even have to work to your benefit. In fact some of your best opportunities are birthed of those very instances. They are those limitation or restrictions set in advance to guide, push, and catapult you into your God given purpose. Before understanding this spiritual truth there were times in my life that I tried to hold onto things and situations because I was determined to make what I had form into what God had shown me would come to pass. There were even people who I tried to hold on to and when they left it hurt deeper than words can express. However God showed me that it was his will for material and relationship doors to close. He later revealed to me that those things and people would have been a burden to my destiny. Excessive and damaging weight that would have slowed down my progress and hindered the manifestation of the vision. You may be there, holding on to people, places, and things, because they are familiar and comfortable. However you must hear from God and determine if they are a part of where he is taking you or are they roadblocks causing you to slow down, detour, or stop completely. We have to find a way to be in tune with God and know that he is working with and for us to manifest our purpose. This is essential, because without this communication or understanding we will have the tendency to become bitter or discouraged. There is nothing more frustrating for a human being than being disconnected from God. We were born to be connected to him, to feel what he feels, to know what he knows, and to see what he sees. To be separated from him is a dark and lonely place that is full of confusion and rather than making life happen life happens to you. We have to be in a place that we are so connected to God that we can sense his move, be connected to his passion, and without a doubt know what his will is. Your destiny depends upon your connectivity to God. There are events or a course of events that will inevitably happen in the course of your life that have the formula for promise embedded into them. They are neatly woven together to knit you the garment of praise and promise. Your destiny includes your overall circumstances or conditions in this life that must work together for your benefit. God will not make you follow his plan for your life. He knows what you need to hear him clearly and he is well aware of what circumstances (limits) will most likely open you up to his presence. But we have to do our part which includes tapping into that part of us that has the ability to connect with him. Look at Hebrews 12:1 "Wherefore seeing we also are compassed about with so great a cloud of witnesses, let us lay aside every weight, and the sin which doth so easily beset us, and let us run with patience the race that is set before us". In Hebrews chapter eleven there is given a list of most honorable acts of faith and accomplishments. These people were totally connected to God and trusted him for the impossible even if it appeared that their act of faith could prove detrimental. Well as great as they were and as wonderful as their accomplishment were they will not compare to the greatness that is within you. In fact they are surrounding us in the spiritual realm as witness to the greatness of God and what he is able to accomplish within the life of faithful men and women who dare to hear and respond to him. We are also instructed to rid ourselves of any and all distractions that could possibly block or hinder us from experiencing and seeing the fulfillment of promise within us. The writer tells us to lay aside not one but every weight. Another word for weight is hindrance. For us to experience the fulfillment of destiny we must give our due diligence to get the things that hinder our progress out of the way. Many times this can be as simple as establishing a list of priorities that is inspired by God and sticking to the list so that you are not distracted from what your kingdom assignment is.

What Your Enemy Hates—and Why You Win

Hell's envy is aimed at image and authority. You bear the image (Genesis 1:26) and you carry the authority of the Second Adam (Matthew 28:18–20). That is why the warfare is personal, but it is also why the victory is settled. Christ disarmed principalities (Colossians 2:15), destroyed the works of the devil (1 John 3:8), and made a public spectacle of darkness. We don't fight for victory; we fight from victory.

Key reality: the cross is the devil's defeat; the resurrection is the Church's authority; Pentecost is the Church's power.

Ordered Steps, Limited Enemy

You highlighted kuwn—God "orders/establishes" our steps (Psalm 37:23). Ordered steps mean bounded opposition. Even in Job's trial, Satan's reach had a leash (Job 1:12; 2:6). Your chapter rightly ties proorizo (predestine) to "limit in advance." God has set boundaries around the battle and grace within the boundary for you to overcome (1 Corinthians 10:13). Closed doors, delays, and holy "no's" are not rejection; they're redirection—guardrails that keep you on the fastest route to promise.

How the Overcomer Walks: Five Practices

1. Armor Up Daily (Ephesians 6:10–18).

- Truth fastens what would otherwise fall apart.
- Righteousness guards your heart from condemnation and compromise.
- Gospel readiness keeps you moving; stagnant feet become targeted feet.
- Faith shield quenches "what if" darts and "it's too late" lies.
- Salvation helmet disciplines your thought life.
- Word of God (rhema)—speak the specific Scripture the Spirit highlights.
- All-prayer is the air support of every battle.

2. Resist and Replace (James 4:7; 2 Corinthians 10:4–5). Submit to God → resist the devil → he flees. Replace enemy narratives with covenant truth. Pull down strongholds (entrenched thought patterns) and replace them with Scripture-formed thinking.

3. Use the Name, the Blood, and Your Testimony (Revelation 12:11). Overcome by the blood of the Lamb (legal grounds), the word of your testimony (spoken agreement), and a cross-formed life (yielded will).

4. Discern Seasons and Exits. Not every fight is yours; some are exits. Ask, "Is this a battle or a boundary?" Many weights disappear when we accept God's no as protection. Maintain Covenant Community (Hebrews 12:1; 10:24–25).
The "great cloud of witnesses" and present-day saints call out courage in you. Isolation amplifies accusation; community reinforces identity.

Reading the Battle Map: Signs You're Under Attack

- Accusation loops (Revelation 12:10): persistent "you're not enough," "you missed it" narratives. Answer with Romans 8:1 and 8:33–34.
- Counterfeit openings: fast, flashy, but peace is absent (Colossians 3:15).
- Fragmented focus: a thousand urgent things—none assigned by God. Go back to your Spirit-given priority list (your own counsel on weights/hindrances).
- Isolation + secrecy: the enemy thrives in the dark. Bring it to light; the power breaks.

When Closed Doors Are Deliverance

You wrote: "Those things and people would have been a burden to my destiny." Amen. Sometimes God answers your prayer to be used by Him by closing what you tried to keep open. Joseph didn't miss destiny because of betrayal; betrayal positioned destiny. Paul's prison bars produced epistles that outlasted his journeys. Closed doors can be conduits.

Ask two questions when a door shuts:

1. What is God protecting me from?
2. What assignment is He protecting through me?

Authority Posture: Standing, Not Striving

- Stand (Ephesians 6:13): The command is repeated—"that ye may be able to stand." Standing is not passivity; it's planted authority.

- Bind/Loose (Matthew 16:19; 18:18): Forbid what Heaven forbids; permit what Heaven permits, in alignment with Scripture.
- Command, don't negotiate (Luke 4:36): Jesus rebuked, silenced, and expelled. Your authority is delegated, not invented—so use His words.

Sample daily decree:

In Jesus 'name, I renounce every lie and accusation. I bind confusion and release clarity. I forbid cycles of distraction and permit divine focus. I stand under the blood, within ordered steps, and I advance only by the Spirit's bidding. Amen.

Discernment in Desires

You noted James 1:14—desire can detour destiny. Add this grid:

- Source: Is the desire springing from intimacy with God or insecurity?
- Season: Is it the right thing at the wrong time? (Song of Songs 2:7—"do not awaken love until it pleases.")
- Stewardship: Will this increase or dilute my assignment?
- Scripture: Does it harmonize with the Word and confirmed counsel?

When desire passes this grid, pursue boldly. If not, release it quickly.

When You Feel Outmatched

Remember your threefold edge:

1. Identity: Image-bearer, adopted child (Romans 8:15–17).
2. Authority: Commissioned ambassador (2 Corinthians 5:20).
3. Anointing: Spirit-empowered witness (Acts 1:8).

The devil traffics in intimidation (Goliath-style taunts), but intimidation collapses against revelation. One word from God outweighs a thousand threats from the enemy.

Reflection & Activation

1. Weights List: What three "weights" (habits, obligations, voices) consistently slow your obedience? Write, renounce, replace.
2. Battle Verse: Which Scripture will you wield this week as your rhema? (Pick one for mind, one for mouth.)
3. Boundary Blessing: Identify one closed door and thank God specifically for the protection it provided.
4. Assignment Focus: Name your top two Kingdom priorities this quarter. Schedule time for them before anything else.

Prayer

Father, I thank You that I am created in Your image and called to overcome. Order my steps, expose every tactic of the enemy, and strengthen me to stand. I put on Your armor, take up the shield of faith, and wield the sword of the Spirit. By the blood of Jesus, I renounce accusation and embrace my authority in Christ. Let every closed door become divine redirection, and every battle become testimony. I agree with Your limits set in advance and Your victory settled from the cross. In Jesus 'name, Amen.

~ 10 ~

PART V – LIVING IN REVELATION

~ 11 ~

EXPERIENCE GREAT & MIGHTY THINGS

"Call unto me, and I will answer thee, and show thee great and mighty things, which thou knowest not." — Jeremiah 33:3

In the book of Jeremiah 33:3 God challenges us to call unto Him and He will respond by showing us Great and Mighty things that we do not know. Think about the gravity of that statement and promise. God is willing to reveal to us things that have either escaped us or been hidden from us for years. These things, these revelations, and these secrets will position us to live in the greatness of God while here on the earth. It is the plan and the will of God for us to be "FREE". Now to fully appreciate this we must fully understand and embrace what it means to be free. Take a look with me in the book of John chapter 8. In verses 31 and 32 He explains that if we continue in his word, then are we his disciples indeed and we will know the truth, and the truth shall make us free. The transliteration of "Free" in the first part of verse 36 is (eleutheroo) which means to cause liberation and to make exempt from the liability of being and doing wrong. But please do not miss what comes next; the second instance of "Free" in the same verse comes from the transliteration (eleutheros), which means we are unrestrained to go at pleasure as a Kingdom Citizen. That is absolutely life changing! God wants us to live a life full of pleasure and no longer bound by the curse and slavery of sin and flesh.

Now let's go back to the Garden again for a moment that we may learn a lesson about this Kingdom Citizen Freedom. Look at Genesis chapter 2 and verse 9, notice that God refers to trees that were very nice to look upon and were good for food, but He also refers to two other trees. Those two trees include "The Tree of Life" and "The Tree of the knowledge of Good and Evil". God never told them that they could not enjoy the tree of "Life", but to at all cost avoid the tree of the knowledge of good and evil (see verse 17). This is very enlightening because God was perfectly okay with them enjoying life, in fact Jesus reiterates that by telling us that he came to give us life in abundance (John 10:10). God wants us to be free to go after life and to help others live life and to be able to do it without being weighed down by the weight and sin which gets us of track. Jesus came to deliver us from this debt of sin and shame and interestingly enough Adam and Eve enjoyed this same covering as they lived with God in the Garden. They did not know anything other than living with God in abundance with every need supplied and enjoying the joy of the lord God being full in their lives. Think about it even in our regenerated lives we are instructed to live life as new creatures, forgetting what is behind us and reaching for what is before us. For years I have heard people refer to the fall of man in the Garden only referring to the fruit, but it is deeper than that. It was humanity wanting to know about what God was protecting them from that caused them to fall into their own shame of sin. When you are partaking in life you are only focused on the goodness of God and what his life for you has to offer. However when you begin to focus on what makes you evil (that is your flesh) and who helps you to be evil (that is the devil) you begin to see your nakedness, shame, weakness, and it causes you to move away from God. You lose your ability to perceive the greatness of God in you. This is why Paul gives us a list of things that our mind should always be on in Philippians chapter 4:8-9. He says if we think on these things the God of peace will be with us. The Perceptual Stimuli that comes from the Holy Spirit will fill your mind with the Good Things that God has for you so much so that you do not have time to think on anything negative. You will not even entertain the presence of the devil or the evil in this earth. In the book of James chapter 4:7 it says "Submit yourselves therefore to God. Resist the devil, and he will flee from you. The devil hates for you to ignore him as if he did not exist. Because the more you do the more he loses his ability to conform your mind into substandard living and senseless distractions. The transliteration of "Resist" is very interesting. It is (anthistemi) from the root word (anti), which means opposite, instead of, and because of but rarely in addition to. Your ability to perceive the plans that God has for you comes from the "Knowledge of Life". This is why Jeremiah writes in Jer. 29:11 "For I know the thoughts that I think toward you, saith the Lord, thoughts of peace, and not of evil, to give you an expected end". When you are so consumed by the unction of God it causes everything related to the devil to flee from your presence. God wants you to "Live" in "Revelation Knowledge". Look at Ephesians 3:3a "How that by revelation he made known unto me the mystery....). He goes on to say in Ephesians 3:9 "And to make all men "SEE" what is the fellowship of the mystery, which from the beginning of the world hath been "HID" in God, who created all things by Jesus Christ". He wants to show you things that have been hidden. He wants you to be able to "Perceive" his plan, how you fit in it, and what you should do. If you have confessed Jesus to be your "Lord", meaning that he is in charge of your life and actions and you believe in your heart that God raised him from the dead, salvation is always sealed by the Holy Spirit of Promise (Ephesians 1:13). Allow that spirit to guide you to all truths. John 14:17 "Even the Spirit of truth; whom the world cannot receive, because it seeth him not, neither knoweth him: but ye know him; for he dwelleth with you, and shall be in you." To my regenerated brothers and sister in Christ Jesus, the Holy Spirit lives in you and he is ready and able to lead you in a way that you can perceive what God is doing and going to do in your life. Allow your journey to begin today. Do not miss out on what God has ready for you to both experience and enjoy. God is ready and willing to unveil the plan to your so that your level of expectation can raised to meet the great heights of the miracles ordained for your life.

Calling, Answering, Unveiling: The Crescendo of a Kingdom Life

Jeremiah 33:3 is not a slogan—it is a summons. "Call to Me... I will answer... and show you great and mighty things." In Hebrew, great and mighty implies hidden, fortified realities—truths kept behind gates, inaccessible by human effort, but opened to those who call. Your journey through this book has been training your spirit to call with clarity, perceive with purity, and walk with authority.

- Call = Invitation issued.
- Answer = Presence encountered.
- Show = Revelation imparted.
- Do = Destiny enacted.

This is the arc of "Perceptual Stimuli." God awakens your spiritual senses, aligns your inner ear to His frequency, and ushers you into rooms of insight where blueprints are handed out, strategies are whispered, and impossible doors swing open.

Freedom That Feels Like Flight

Jesus 'double use of free (John 8:31–36) is your liftoff sequence:

- Eleutheroo — you are liberated from guilt, penalty, and bondage.
- Eleutheros — you are released to move freely as a Kingdom citizen, unrestrained by fear or shame.

Freedom in Christ is not only release from what binds; it is promotion into what God intends. You are not merely forgiven; you are authorized. Your liberty is not a hallway—it's a runway.

The Tree You're Invited to Enjoy

From Eden to Calvary, God's intention has never changed: choose Life. The tragedy of Eden was not curiosity; it was a misdirected focus—attention traded from Life to "knowing" evil. When your gaze drifts from the Giver to the garbage, shame strides in, and perception dims.

The Spirit is recalibrating your focus. "Think on these things" (Philippians 4:8) is not denial; it is dominion. You fill the mind with what Heaven is saying, and the God of peace stands guard over your heart and thoughts. In that atmosphere, the enemy is starved of attention and forced to flee (James 4:7). Resistance (anthistemi) looks like choosing the opposite narrative—truth instead of torment, promise instead of panic, assignment instead of distraction.

Revelation Knowledge: Where Hidden Things Become Highways

Ephesians 3 unveils God's desire: not only to reveal mystery but to make all men see. Revelation is sight for the spirit—eyes enlightened, paths illumined, timing clarified. In revelation, confusion loses jurisdiction. You won't merely know His will; you will recognize it when it arrives and move with it as it unfolds.

This is how "Perceptual Stimuli" becomes movement—revelation births direction, direction births obedience, obedience births outcomes that look like miracles.

The Spirit Within: Your Forever Guide

Saved, sealed, and Spirit-indwelt (Ephesians 1:13), you are not navigating by instinct but by indwelling Presence. The Spirit of Truth (John 14:17) doesn't just inform—He forms Christ in you. He tutors your attention, disciplines your desires, and cultivates a reflex of Yes, Lord.

Let this be your final chapter resolve: I will live led. Led in prayer. Led in purpose. Led in generosity. Led in holiness. Led in boldness. Led into great and mighty things prepared beforehand that I should walk in them (Ephesians 2:10).

A Final Sweep: What This Journey Has Forged in You

- Identity: Created in His image, carriers of His breath, ambassadors of His Kingdom.
- Discernment: Trained senses that hear shama—intelligent listening that yields immediate obedience.
- Courage: Willingness to step out of the boat when bid, to treat urgency as holy, to prize presence over comfort.
- Authority: More than conquerors, born to overcome, armored to stand, commissioned to bind and loose.
- Favor: Surrounded as with a shield, positioned at God's doorposts, living in repairing grace and unsearchable riches.
- Transfer: Ready to steward resources heaven redirects for Kingdom outcomes.
- Destiny: Pressing toward the mark—because the promises are Yes and Amen.

Everything has led to this: a life that expects and experiences the great and mighty.

Five Practices to Live the Finale Daily

1. Call & Record. Begin each morning with Jeremiah 33:3. Ask God for one "great and mighty" insight. Write it. Revelation unused becomes revelation unfelt.
2. Pray Your Identity. Declare who you are in Christ (Ephesians 1; Romans 8). Confidence in identity quiets a thousand counterfeit invitations.
3. Move on Peace. Let the peace of Christ umpire your decisions (Colossians 3:15). If peace withdraws, pause. If peace persists, proceed.
4. Choose the Life Tree. Curate your attention. Replace doom-scroll with Word-dwell. Feed your mind what fuels your mission.
5. Testify in Motion. Share weekly "perception → obedience → outcome" testimonies. Your story trains others to perceive and obey.

Declarations for a Great & Mighty Life

Speak these aloud:

- I call, and the Lord answers me; He shows me great and mighty things I do not know.
- I am free indeed—liberated and released to move as a Kingdom citizen.
- My mind is set on what is true, noble, just, pure, lovely, and praiseworthy; the God of peace is with me.
- I resist the devil by agreeing with God; the enemy flees from my life, my family, and my assignment.

- The Spirit of Truth dwells in me and leads me into all truth—today I recognize, respond, and rejoice.
- I walk in favor as with a shield; doors open, wisdom flows, resources align for Kingdom purpose.
- I will see the goodness of the Lord in the land of the living; my expectations are high because His promises are sure.
- I live to display His glory—on earth as it is in Heaven.

Climactic Commissioning

In Jesus 'name, step over the threshold. This is the sound of gates unlocking. This is the sight of paths appearing where there were none. This is the feel of chains dropping with a final clatter. You were not preserved to play small; you were prepared to partner with God.

From this day, call boldly, listen wholly, obey quickly, and walk freely. Let "Perceptual Stimuli" be more than a theme—let it be your life pattern: Spirit-stirred perception, Scripture-shaped interpretation, faith-filled action, and glory-giving testimony.

The Kingdom is not waiting for better conditions; it is waiting for bolder participation—yours.

Closing Prayer

Father, in the name of Jesus, I answer Your invitation to call. Open my eyes to behold great and mighty things. Liberate me from every residue of shame, and release me into the free movement of a Kingdom citizen. Tune my ears to Your whisper, align my steps to Your order, and set my heart ablaze for Your purpose. Let the Spirit of Truth fill and lead me—today and every day—into revelation, obedience, and fruitfulness. I receive the mantle to perceive and the courage to perform. Make my life a sign of Your goodness in the land of the living. I expect miracles, I embrace assignments, and I exalt Jesus. Amen.

EPILOGUE: FROM PERCEPTION TO PERMANENCE

You have been equipped to discern and demonstrate. Keep calling. Keep seeing. Keep stepping. The God who promised great and mighty things will meet you in the middle of your obedience with outcomes only Heaven could author.

Now go—experience great and mighty things.

Dr. Tony Medley Sr. is a pastor, teacher, mentor, and author whose life and ministry have been dedicated to helping people discover the power of God's Word spoken over their lives. Known for his passionate preaching and practical teaching, Dr. Medley has spent decades equipping believers to hear God's voice, walk in their identity in Christ, and live with purpose and bold faith. His ministry extends beyond the pulpit—through books, training materials, stage plays, and discipleship resources—designed to ignite transformation in individuals, churches, and communities.

Dr. Medley combines deep biblical insight with everyday application, ensuring that readers not only understand the Scriptures but also live them out with confidence. With a message that is both prophetic and practical, Dr. Medley inspires people to see themselves through heaven's perspective. He believes every person is "wrapped in the conversation" of God and destined to thrive in His promises.

When he is not writing or teaching, Dr. Medley is serving his church family, mentoring emerging leaders, and enjoying time with his own family, who remain his greatest earthly joy.